HOW TO ATTRACT GOOD LUCK

T0145906

Also available in the Condensed Classics Library

HOW TO ATTRACT GOOD LUCK

by A.H.Z. Carr

The Unparalleled Classic On Lucky Living

Abridged and Introduced
by Mitch Horowitz

THE CONDENSED CLASSICS LIBRARY™

Published by Gildan Media LLC
aka G&D Media.
www.GandDmedia.com

How to Attract Good Luck was originally published in 1952
G&D Media Condensed Classics edition published 2018
Abridgement and Introduction copyright © 2016 by Mitch
Horowitz

FIRST EDITION: 2018

Cover design by David Rheinhardt of Pyrographx

Interior design by Meghan Day Healey of Story Horse, LLC.

ISBN: 978-1-7225-0050-4

CONTENTS

Good Luck Is No Accident

D o you want good luck? Of course you do. We all depend, to one degree or another, on fortuitous opportunities to put our skills to use, to meet people who provide vital openings for us, and to discover information that makes a crucial difference in our lives.

You are about to experience a condensation of one of the most intriguing and little-known books in the self-help tradition: *How to Attract Good Luck*. The book offers a straightforward and ethical recipe for cultivating your ability to identify and prepare for those crucial moments where life's currents lift you, or at least help you along. The title *How to Attract Good Luck* may sound like it belongs to a gambling guide. But this book is the furthest thing from it.

Economist, journalist, and diplomat A.H.Z. Carr wrote *How to Attract Good Luck* in 1952. Carr had served as an economic adviser in the presidential administrations of Franklin Roosevelt and Harry Truman, and spent time on economic and diplomatic missions in Europe and the Far East. He amassed a great deal of experience observing how most personal misfortune arises from impetuous, shortsighted, or unethical behavior. By "luck" Carr was referring not to blind chance but rather to how we can bend circumstances to our favor through specific patterns of behavior.

In an entertaining and incisive fashion, his book catalogues the insights he gleaned on how *virtue pays*. In a certain sense, Carr's book is really a guide to honorable living, which, in his estimation, pays dividends in success, stability, and peace of mind. Carr's work is an exegesis of a statement attributed to scientist Louis Pasteur: "Chance favors the prepared mind." Preparation, in Carr's view, is based not only in rigor and study, but also in a kind of personal comportment that makes one ready to take authority or act decisively when the need arises.

In an age where people gobble up copies of blatantly amoral success guides like *The 48 Laws to Power*, I find something distinctly appealing and rock-solid in Carr's work. This is a self-help book that can be used by someone who tries to live by the Beatitudes or the Boy Scouts Code of Honor. And why *wouldn't* we want to live by enduring guides to decency and ethic solidity? Carr tells us, in effect, that we can both achieve in the world and remain appealing as people. In fact, he maintains, very persuasively, that sound behavior and achievement are intimately united. Do you doubt that? Put his ideas to the test.

Without sardonicism or irony, I wish you a heartfelt *good luck*.

—Mitch Horowitz

Chapter One

Chance Versus Luck

People have always sought ways to improve their luck. Their efforts have generally centered around portents, omens, and black magic. The Roman augur, interpreting the flights of birds, has been succeeded in modern times by numerologists and clairvoyants. But these practices have degraded the subject of luck. At the very mention of the word, many intelligent people understandably lift a skeptical eyebrow.

But our understanding of luck can be lifted from a black-cat level to an infinitely higher and broader plane. Psychology has opened the gate to a new and rational approach to luck. Armed with modern insights, those who seek can discover the true nature of luckiness. Luck is not a mere matter of poker winnings and the like but rather a *specific condition of mind*. This book shows how the lucky condition of mind can be attained.

At the outset, we must clarify the difference between "chance" and "luck." Chance comprises the infinite number of unpredictable happenings, both great and trivial, that are constantly at work in the world, whether a volcanic eruption or a sparrow's flight. Most of the chances we perceive in life seem remote and meaningless. But now and then a chance will touch the interests of an individual—and then it becomes very personal and significant indeed. *For as soon as human emotions are affected by a chance, it has been transformed into luck.* Luck, then, is the effect of chance on our lives.

But—and this is of vital importance—chance is not the only element in luck. Another factor is involved—ourselves. For it is our *response* to chance that provides the counterpoint in the harmony of events that we call luck. Whether and how a chance affects us is largely determined by our own attitude and behavior. Chance and response, between them, provide the warp and woof of existence, and the pattern of every life.

The central theme of this book is: *We can improve our luck by making ourselves readier for the chances of life as they come to us.* Shakespeare put it this way: "If it be not now, yet it will come. The readiness is all." These words have profound meaning. For the vigor of effort that we make to be ready for luck may well be the deciding factor between a lucky and unlucky life.

It lies within our power to influence, not chance, but our relation to chance. And in that sense none of us can escape a measure of responsibility for his own luck.

CHAPTER TWO

How Zest Exposes Us to Luck

Good luck usually strikes into the world of men with the suddenness of lightening. How can we attract this beneficent lightening in our lives?

Over many years hundreds of people have told me their stories of good luck. More than half of them had one thing in common: the lucky episode began for the person concerned at a time when he was exposed to others—*when someone else unexpectedly said something important to him*. Most of our good luck—the beneficial effect of chance upon our lives—comes to us through other people. To expose ourselves to luck, then, means in essence to come into healthy human relationships with more people. The more luck-lines a person throws out, the more luck he is likely to find.

A high proportion of lucky chances comes to us through strangers, or people we know only slightly.

This is not really surprising. Most of our well-worn contacts rarely offer us a new perspective, or a new piece of important information. But displaying "unexpected friendlessness" toward people we do not know is the secret of much of the luck of life. Ancient myths and parables repeatedly tell of rewards heaped upon someone who is kind to a travelling stranger—only to discover that the seeming stranger is a god or angel.

Of course, not every stranger merits our trust. We must guard against the aggressive bore, the gossip, or the ruthless peddler. But do not allow fear or indifference to block you off to the potential luck of The Stranger.

In enabling us to throw out luck-lines to strangers and old acquaintances alike, one quality has almost magical power—the quality of zest. Philosopher Bertrand Russell has called zest "the most universal and distinctive mark of happy men." Zest is also the mark of most lucky men—a quality which, in the struggle of life, often overshadows and outweighs serious character flaws and limitations of mind.

Never confuse zest with greed or gluttony. Zest means to take an explorer's interest in the world. The zestful person upon meeting others is curious not what they may think of him, how much money they make, or what they can do for him. Rather, he wants to discover their personalities and ways of life. He is capable of sincere enthusiasm, praise, and appreciation. The zestful person may feel angered or disquieted by events, but he loves life in all its follies. We need zest to counteract feelings of anxiety, which lay waste to human relationships.

Experimentation of almost any kind leads to zest. So does the discovery of a meaningful avocation or hobby—any well-defined core activity that stimulates thought and beckons new skill.

Frequently the things we read with zest are coupled directly with strokes of luck. Even a sentence or two, found by chance, can set off a train of lucky events. This is why books have a special place in luck development. The effort of attention needed to read a book, and especially a book with serious content, impresses it strongly on the memory, so that its ideas can be readily evoked by passing chance and brought into lucky use.

Chapter Three

How Generosity Invites Luck

Some people put out luck-lines that get them nowhere. Things may start out all right but they find that instead of good luck they have been tempting misfortune. Sometimes we reach out to people—but our *unchecked* ego gets in our way.

Probably no human frailty is more likely to bring bad luck than an exaggerated need for appreciation. This unhappy state of mind, which usually grows out of a rooted feeling of insecurity, drives its victim to advertise his importance and demand that the busy world pay attention to him. The egotist tends to be inattentive when others are talking, he causes acquaintances to take a passive position in conversation and to therefore withhold valuable information and ideas. Even more serious, such a person tends to brag and boast, if sometimes in subtle and indirect ways.

The chronic egotist is always a candidate for bad luck. But the strong characteristic opposite to egotism, generosity of spirit, consistently acts as a magnet for favorable chances.

Note that we're speaking of *uncalculated generosity*. A distinction should also be drawn between genuine generosity and the compulsive and almost frantic displays of giving which some neurotic people make.

The luck that comes to us as a result of true generosity seldom takes the form of spectacular, immediate blessings out the blue. The real reward of the generous is invisible and secret. It lies partly in their own psychological health and partly in the hearts of others—in the reservoir of good will they build up. The generous person creates an unsuspected potential of good luck that needs only a touch from chance to burst all at once into happy reality.

In luck-development we need to keep in mind this seemingly obvious yet easily neglected fact: *In order to have real friends, a man must be capable of being one.* We can, for example, try a little hard to understand the problems of a friend, and give him such assistance as we're able without seeking return. When a friend is suffering, we can suppress remarks that would only add to his pain. Likewise, when a friend is fortunate, we can fight down our envy and try to enter his gladness.

The key point is that *every act of true friendship and generosity is proof of a rising luck-potential within us.*

Chapter Four

Turning Points

It is actually possible to anticipate favorable chances. Chance, which produces the effects in our lives that we call luck, has its own way of behaving. We need to become aware of two marked tendencies in the fall of chance: *rhythm* and *interconnection*.

Chance follows the same rhythm of nature. It is not an even, unbroken rhythm. We can learn to expect the alternation of runs of chance; moreover we can learn to expect it more at certain times than others. *The runs of chance in life are normally short.* After similar chances have appeared in succession several times, we have every reason to expect a change. This calls for expectancy and alertness.

As the rhythm of chance often points to the turning points of life, so does the characteristic that I have called *interconnection*. From time to time, two or more interlocking chances in close succession touch almost every life. And it is at these points where luck reveals its power most dramatically. At such times, by alertness, we can often "pyramid" our luck, using the luck of the first chance as a steppingstone to the greater luck of the others.

It is a fact of many, and perhaps most lives, that large fulfillments come not at a steady pace but by sudden leaps. After a single lucky chance we are wise to keep all of our senses alert for other chances that may interlock with the first, and provide a major turning point of life. The conscious effort to be alert to chance seems especially productive of turning points in periods of pronounced social change, when the old order is upturned.

Enthusiasm for the spectacular and impatience with the commonplace chances of life are likely to result in peaks of good luck alternating with deep valleys of misfortune. The reservoir of luck in each of us is far more often tapped by chance in frequent little jets than in big bursts.

We must also keep alert in the face of *crucial chances*. To do so we need to maintain our physical energy at a high level. A sound regimen of diet, sleep, and exercise, helps assure the ability of our alertness and mental acuity. Beyond this, we can generate alertness through *imaginative anticipation*. Obviously we cannot anticipate all eventualities, but we can often decide in advance what we shall do if certain common chances befall us.

Finally, when the occurrence of a chance seems fairly probable, a single preparatory action can go far to maintain the essential alertness until the event takes place.

CHAPTER FIVE

Our Desires and Our Luck

There is no reason to believe that opportunity knocks only once; but whether it knocks once, twice, or ten times, only the self-knowing mind, the mind that knows what it wants and what it will risk, is likely to recognize the real nature of the chance and act accordingly. Often the claims of competing desires are so strong as to make a decision difficult. No matter how complex the problem presented by chance, a firm set of values for our various desires helps us to find the lucky answer.

By testing chances against our personal values we sometimes perceive luck where others would see none. By knowing what you really want in life, you may detect opportunities that others may not understand or value.

Here is a core principle of life: *The person who knows the relative importance, for himself, of conflicting desires is best prepared to recognize the favorable chance as it passes, and to transform it into luck.* It is not easy to prioritize your desires, but it is absolutely vital if you want to bring more luck into your life. Fortunately, modern psychology has greatly clarified this problem. It tells us that a person's desires are not fixed and rigid; rather, they are malleable, ever-changing, and evolving in us from cradle to grave.

As adults we have ten basic, universal desires:

1. Love, both romantic and the affections of friends and family.
2. Procreation, with the urge to sex, marriage, and children.
3. Group status, or a firm place in the community or group.
4. Prestige, or recognition by others of our talents and distinctions.
5. Economic security and a satisfying standard of living.
6. Self-respect, or a sense of living up to meritorious standards of behavior.
7. Self-expression, or the use of one's abilities and talents.
8. Faith, or belief in a universal purpose or goal outside ourselves.

9. Long life, specifically the prospect of long-term physical and mental vigor.
10. Good health and freedom from illness.

The evaluation of desires is a highly personal matter. Everyone has, in effect, a private blend of desires. Some want more love than others, some more prestige, some more economic security, and so on. This difference profoundly affects our ideas of what is lucky. We must also distinguish honestly between basic desires versus compulsions or obsessions. Unchecked desires can balloon into obsessions or addictions, which destroy our luck.

CHAPTER SIX

Our Abilities and Our Luck

One of the major elements in appraising the luck-content of a chance can be expressed in the question: *Does it accord with my abilities?* Unless our estimate of our abilities is realistic, we can be tempted by chance into foolhardy and disastrous ventures.

Part of the basic formula for a lucky life is: *Make the most of what you are, and do not try to be more than you can be.* The man who tries to live beyond his capacities, physically, psychologically, or economically, invites misfortune.

The more that you know about the requirements and hazards of a given chance, the more likely you are to find good luck in it, and avoid bad luck—*if you have a realistic understanding of your own abilities and limitations.* Nothing is more promising of good luck than the chance that accords with desire and ability; nothing is more dangerous than chance that appeals to desire but is not backed up by requisite ability.

So long as your judgment is mature and sound, there is a role for *inner conviction* in assessing one's abilities. When internal conviction asserts itself with sufficient power, it can often bring luck in spite of the most adverse judgments.

In sum, only when a given chance conforms both to basic desire and to demonstrated or indicated ability does it give genuine promise of good luck.

CHAPTER SEVEN

Judgment as an Element in Luck

Judgment has been called the eye of the mind. When people demonstrate bad judgment it is usually due less to defects in thinking than to emotional factors that have clouded the mind's outlook.

An appalling amount of bad luck can be attributed to three emotional states: boredom, anxiety, and overconfidence. Use these principles to your benefit: 1) Beware of boredom. 2) Allow for anxiety. 3) Overcome overconfidence. These rules are important markers on the road to better luck.

When a person is bored he hungers for an event that will lead to a better life. He looks with favor upon anything that seems to promise a thrill. This makes him highly vulnerable to bad luck because he does not assess the risks of the chances that he takes. Boredom has pushed many people into tragic misfortune.

Similarly in forming our judgment of chances, we must allow for inevitable and natural anxiety. Anxiety can cause us to reject favorable chances, even when they come straight at us, by making us think that we that we see peril and risk where there is none. In order to be lucky, we are not required to give up anxiety (some of which is healthy); but we must make allowances for the appearance of anxiety, and bring our fears to the surface for appropriate judgment.

In some ways, the more important rule for protecting our judgment from unstable emotions is the need to "overcome overconfidence." A dangerous sense of overconfidence can result from: 1) a run of luck, 2) a lack of experience, and 3) a misunderstanding of motive.

We sometimes believe that we understand people's motives when we actually do not. Too many of us accept, at face value, the motives put forward by people with whom we must deal in chance situations. Not that we need to be cynical about the motives of other people. Cynicism is, in truth, only an inverted form of naiveté, twisting one's view of reality. At the same time, when we have no sound reason to believe in the other person's purity of motive, we do well to pause for reflection.

Chapter Eight

Safeguarding Luck with Self-Respect

It is always unlucky to forfeit self-respect. The test of self-respect is especially important when chance demands an instantaneous decision and allows no time for judgment to probe and consider.

It is not always easy to tell which course of action in a complex situation will best maintain self-respect. And, curiously enough, some people even shrug at the term self-respect, failing to realize the decisive role it plays in good luck. They think that enjoying life is the only measure of success. The stifling of conscience, however, means that *the psychic trouble within us seeks other outlets*, such as the warping of the personality through neurotic fear or vicious criticism.

At the same time, there can be no doubt that self-respecting behavior frequently results in strong new luck-lines, over which material benefits flow. For example, the courage displayed by an act of selfless honesty, such as owning up to a serious mistake and not letting others take the fall for it, often marks someone as accountable and deserving of trust with serious responsibilities.

It is never too late to reaffirm self-respect. Fortunately for us, the occasional violence we do to our self-respect *is* only occasional. A single self-respecting action, taken when the personality was in danger of becoming permanently enfeebled, can perform a miracle of regeneration.

At this point a warning should be posted. It is easy to confuse self-respect with pride—and pride is a positively unlucky trait. In contrast to self-respect, pride—whether over origin, beauty, position, achievement, or anything else—is fundamentally an expression of insecurity, with its roots in illusion. It is a sign that someone is trying to cover up a feeling of spiritual weakness by pointing to a superficial advantage or external superiority.

When we sharply separate self-respect from pride and vanity, it serves us best in the selection and rejection of chances.

Chapter Nine

The Intuitive Approach to Luck

B elow the threshold of consciousness is a kind of secret reference library of unspoken knowledge and forgotten impressions. The unconscious mind at certain times will pull out the evidence that bears on a risk before you, delivering its verdict in the mysterious form of *intuition*.

Our intuitive judgments of others may sometimes arise from unconscious impressions of previous experiences with people of similar characteristics. The wife of a friend once cautioned her husband to avoid Jim, a new acquaintance at work. The friend later told me: "Jim was a good fellow, but I felt highly competitive toward him. He brought out the worst in me." The wife had demonstrated sound intuition. No one can afford to forget that while he is influencing other people, they are also influencing him, for better or worse. Getting involved with competitive people often brings bad luck.

Little mishaps in the home or office have many times been preludes to larger misfortunes. This is certainly not to say that we should seek for omens. But there is nothing superstitious about recognizing the implications of our unconscious actions. Sigmund Freud stressed this point, noting: "The Roman who . . . withdrew from an undertaking because he had stumbled on his threshold . . . was a better psychologist than we . . . For his stumbling could demonstrate to him the existence of a doubt . . . the force of which could weaken the power of his intention at the moment of its execution. For only by concentrating all psychic forces on the desired aim can one be assured of its success."

Never confuse intuition with a mere *wish* for something. Apparent intuitions that coincide with feverish wishes, and which involve high risks—such as the desire to romantically win over an uninterested or deeply flawed lover—should always be regarded with suspicion.

The Power of the Response

S ome acts of chance, like a fatal accident, leave no room for response. The vast realm of luck, however, is ruled not by chance alone but jointly, by chance and by ourselves.

Even seeming disasters can be converted or redirected by a sound response, which makes us more educated, more resilient, and more knowledgeable. Sometimes the response may aid us in some other area that seems distant from the event itself.

Underlying the sound responses of lucky people to chance are three predominant character traits: *high energy, vigorous imagination, and strong faith.*

These are the "big three" that can transform raw chance into good fortune. If you are lacking in one or two of these and are willing to try to do something about it, that willingness alone is the gateway to better luck. A vigorous effort to develop ourselves in any lucky direction can itself bring us into closer harmony with chance.

We will now review the importance of each trait, and how to strengthen it.

Chapter Eleven

How Increased Energy Produces Luck

H ere is a statement so obvious that one may easily lose sight of its significance: *Much of our greatest luck comes to us when our energy is high.*

Heightened energy manifests itself to us in a number of specifically luck ways—sometimes in a display of muscular power to meet a sudden chance, but more frequently in a state of mind. Notably, three psychology attitudes are closely linked to luck: *presence of mind, confidence, and determination.*

Presence of mind is a kind of alertness. As soon as we have identified the chance, the alert condition undergoes a profound change. We no longer watch concentratedly for something to happen. It has happened. Our problem now is how to respond. Instead of keeping attention focused entirely on the chance event, we survey our surroundings—we "get the picture"—we see what things or circumstances near us can be of use in responding to the chance. The more "present" our mind is, the more likely we are to respond luckily to the chance.

Confidence is vital to our luck development. Preparation induces confidence. Especially in those instances that involve other people, like your subject if you are a journalist, or your partners if you are an investor. *Preparatory study of the facts makes for luck.* Of course, no one is confident all the time, or in the face of all chances. Our need is to *use periods of high energy to prepare for the chances of life that seem most probable.*

Like confidence and presence of mind, the quality of **determination** is also associated with high energy. Some people are more determined than others because they are able to *renew their energy* in relation to an activity. Often a person has high energy at the outset of a project, but it dissipates. *Determination grows out of the repeated tapping of your energy reserves in the pursuit of a single purpose.* This usually occurs: 1) When you are focused on a definite purpose, and you keep your aim constantly in sight, stimulating hope and renewing incentive. 2) When you prevent yourself from growing stale through an occasional change of activity, which makes possible a zestful return to the attack.

High energy is in large degree the expression of an attitude toward life. "A single successful effort of moral volition," wrote William James, "such as saying 'no' to some habitual temptation, or performing some courageous act, will launch a man on a higher level of energy for days or weeks, will give him a new range of power."

It must also be said that anyone who fails to make an effort to eat and drink wisely, to get enough exercise and rest, and to shake off his worries, greatly weakens his power to respond successfully to life's chances. Any effort we make to raise the level of our energy by improvement in these essential aspects of living automatically tends to improve our luck potential.

Chapter Twelve

Imagination and Luck

Wherever luck is most impressive, it is usually because energy has been directed by imagination, which reveals the potentialities of a chance.

Not every imagination, as we all know, makes for good luck. Notably, the egocentric imagination, which evokes images concerned primarily with selfish gratifications, invites unluckiness. One of its distinguishing products is the *daydream*—the fantasy that is always concerned with the future of the dream and which leads to the fictional fulfillment of some desire. Heedlessly indulged, the daydream can be a menace to good luck. It weakens one's hold on reality and reduces the energy available for the real tasks of life.

Another unlucky way the egocentric imagination expresses itself is morbidity. The morbid imagination tends to focus on the unpleasant perceptions that fit into its dark and distorted picture of life, and to ignore constructive or encouraging elements. Where this condition exists, a trivial chance can easily produce a major increase of unhappiness.

The unmistakable characteristic of the healthy and lucky imagination is that it readily turns outward, away from the self. It does not confuse the world of external reality with the images conjured up by desire or anxiety. The healthy imagination also has a high capacity for empathy, which enables you to share in the feelings of others in given situations. A great part of human luck depends on other people. When we share in their states of mind, we are more likely to respond to chances in ways that link them to us emotionally, making for a greater probability of luck for all concerned.

Just as a strong empathic imagination can bring good luck out of unfavorable circumstances, such as forming a bond with a gifted person who has experienced a temporary setback, a counter weakness area can lead to disastrous failures. This is *irrational prejudice.* Irrational prejudice includes snobbishness, religious or racial bigotry, and class discrimination. The creeping vine of intolerance chokes off the empathic imagination. What's more, prejudice dwells in insecure minds, which are natural targets for trouble.

CHAPTER THIRTEEN

The Luckiness of Faith

The word "faith" is used here, not in the sense of conventional lip service to a religious creed, but to signify the state of mind of those who are either wholly at one with their religion, or who profoundly hold a philosophic belief from which flows an affirmation of life and a moral principle.

Sometimes men and women who have neither religion nor philosophy try to fill this void in their lives by pinning their faith on their children or their work. Love of one's children and respect for one's work can be strengthening influences. They cannot, however, take the psychological place of a profound identification between the self and some large religious or philosophic conviction of good, which provides a moral basis for behavior.

When we lack the steadying power of faith, the insecurity feelings latent in all of us tend to run away with our behavior. A psychologist recently made an informal study among his university students of three negative traits: bragging, snobbishness, and secretiveness, all of which express insecurity. When he correlated the results with what he knew of the students' backgrounds and beliefs, there seemed to be an unmistakable link between the presence of these unlucky flaws and the absence of religious or philosophic faith.

We can cite very specific reasons why luck is most likely to be found in the faith-directed way of life. Faith tends to develop in the individual certain attributes that go far to ensure successful responses to chance. Courage is one of these attributes. But no less important are two traits that are in good part the psychological offspring of faith: *integrity* and *sense of proportion*.

It is through integrity that faith chiefly affects our responses to chance. Not that we find integrity in every person who professes a religion or a philosophy. But whenever we do find a person of genuine integrity, there, almost by definition, we find a core of faith. The exaltation of moral principle manifests a belief in universal law.

Together with courage and integrity, a third lucky characteristic flows from faith—the wide-horizoned attitude of mind that we think of as a *sense of proportion*. This attitude expresses itself in the personality through humility and through humor. The man who sees his actual position in the universe, and who can endure the revelation of his personal unimportance, gains enormous inner strength. Throughout life the sense of proportion links with chance to produce good luck and to mitigate misfortune.

The same quality, the sense of proportion derived from religion or philosophy, has a further bearing on our fortunes through its power in combatting envy, among the unluckiest of human characteristics. Competitive beings that we are, we all experience envy. But if envy is quickly controlled by a sense of proportion, it does little harm. In fact, a feeling of envy may be transformed to admiration and spur you to make more of your abilities. The great polar explorer Amundsen said that when he heard that Commodore Peary had reached the North Pole, his first thought was, "Then I shall visit both Poles." And he did. The danger to luck arises when envy in unchecked and becomes a permanent state of mind, which engenders bitterness, scheming, and cynicism.

The envy-resisting sense of proportion, rooted integrity, and sustained courage—those are stars of luck's constellation; and faith is their parent-quality. The need of effort to develop these attributes is too plain to need much discussion. What must be stressed is the point that any such effort, if it is to succeed, must follow the spiritual and intellectual route toward faith.

CHAPTER FOURTEEN

The Will to Be Lucky

The conscious steering of our actions, which is the peculiar privilege of man, is a skill that must be learned. The successful steersman in life, the lucky man, requires a degree of mastery of difficult arts of behavior and self-expression. Certain specific qualities of character and personality must be developed in us before we can find a lucky way through life.

When men have a keen sense of responsibility for their own fortunes, they can influence their luck far more than they dream. The chances of life, from which luck flows, are a kind of cosmic committee, constantly testing our readiness for membership in the lodge of the lucky. The *will to be lucky* is the crux of our internal development.

To modify destructive habits, which often have strong roots, *we must feel active resentment of the insecurity feelings that push us into inferior patterns of behavior*—and that make us unlucky in life. That gives us the requisite strength of feeling to challenge and change depleting habits of behavior.

Any effort we make, however slight, to prevent the dictation of our behavior by insecurity feelings is a step toward luckiness. A single modest improvement at a time is often enough to produce far-reaching consequences in one's fortunes. We have examined the importance to our luck of a number of characteristics which have a close relationship to the workings of chance: zest and generosity, with the power to attract luck into our lives; alertness, self-knowledge, judgment, self-respect, and intuition—all of high value in the recognition of favorable chances; and qualities of special significance in our responses to chance—energy, with its bearing on the presence of mind, confidence, and determination—imagination—and courage, sense of proportion, and integrity, which grow out of faith.

By doing a few relatively simple things over a period of a few months, you can often develop the lucky side of your personality to an extent that can seem miraculous. Vast and ungovernable is the power of chance; and yet, as we have seen, its influence on our luck is profoundly shaped by our own actions. The presence of this book is itself a chance, and your response to it may go far to affect your fortune to come.

CHAPTER FIFTEEN

Lucky Habits: Takeaway Points

In order to retain the material we've covered in this book, here are gleanings to consider:

- Demonstrate "unexpected friendliness" to colleagues, strangers, or casual acquaintances. In the history of religion and myth, displays of unwarranted hospitality or friendliness often prove the turning point that results in rewards being showered on someone who unknowingly aids an angel, the gods, or a disguised royal.

- Pursue topics or lines of work for which you feel zest. This is a recipe for fortuitous connections and relationships.

- Boredom is a harbinger of bad luck. Boredom leads you to rash or frivolous actions in pursuit of relief and excitement. Stay busy and engaged.

- Generosity is almost always rewarded one way or another.

- Watch for "small chances" to accomplish your aims. A small step either in conjunction with other small steps or by itself can produce unexpected results.

- Stay alert for larger "critical chances"—be watchful.

- It is lucky to know what we want. Focus brings us right action.

- Never imagine yourself more formidable or skilled than you really are. Be realistic about your current level of abilities and where they must grow.

- Healthful self-respect keeps you out of trouble.

- Avoid hyper-competitive colleagues and acquaintances. Those who make us feel competitive easily can tempt us into unlucky displays of egotism.

- Always look for how to turn chance events into good use.

- William James wrote: "A single successful effort of moral volition, such as saying 'no' to some habitual temptation, or performing some courageous act, will launch a man on a higher level of energy for days or weeks, will give him a new range of power."

- Prejudice brings bad luck.

- Ethical courage, not impulsiveness or truculence, imbues you with nobility. Defending a loved one is almost always a lucky act.

- Acting without integrity invites misfortune.

- Envy moves you to foolish actions and pettiness. It is the bug zapper of good luck.

- Any effort we make, however slight, to prevent the dictation of our behavior by insecurity feelings is a step toward luckiness.

ABOUT THE AUTHORS

Born in Chicago in 1902, A.H.Z. CARR was an economic adviser to the presidential administrations of Franklin Roosevelt and Harry Truman, and participated in economic and diplomatic missions in Western Europe and East Asia. He also served as a consulting economist to several large corporations. Carr wrote for magazines including *Harper's, Reader's Digest*, and *The Saturday Evening Post*. He died in 1971.

MITCH HOROWITZ, who abridged and introduced this volume, is the PEN Award-winning author of books including *Occult America* and *The Miracle Club: How Thoughts Become Reality*. *The Washington Post* says Mitch "treats esoteric ideas and movements with an even-handed intellectual studiousness that is too often lost in today's raised-voice discussions." Follow him @MitchHorowitz.